START-UP
GEOGRAPHY

JOBS
PEOPLE DO

Anna Lee

Evans

Published by Evans Brothers Limited
2A Portman Mansions
Chiltern Street
London W1U 6NR

Produced for Evans Brothers Limited by
White-Thomson Publishing Ltd.
2/3 St Andrew's Place
Lewes, East Sussex BN7 1UP

Printed in Hong Kong by Wing Ting Tong Co. Ltd.

Editor: Elaine Fuoco-Lang
Consultants: Lorraine Harrison, Senior Lecturer in
Geography Education at the University of Brighton
and Christine Bentall, Key Stage One teacher at
St Bartholomew's Church of England Primary
School, Brighton.
Designer: Tessa Barwick

Cover: All photographs by Alan Towse

British Library Cataloguing in Publication Data
Lee, Anna
    Jobs people do. - (Start-up geography)
    1.Occupations - Juvenile literature
    I.Title
    331.7

ISBN: 0 237 52462 7

Acknowledgements:
The publishers would like to thank staff, students and
parents at Coldean Primary School, Brighton, for their
involvement in the preparation of this book.

Picture Acknowledgements:
All photographs by Alan Towse except Hodder Wayland
Picture Library (Dana Smillie) 10 *(left);* WTPix 12 *(left);*
Hodder Wayland Picture Library 13 *(bottom);*
Christopher Cormack/Impact 14 *(bottom);*
Gavin Milverton/Impact 15 *(left).*

Contents

People who work at our school 4

People who help us learn 6

Around our school 8

Our local area 10

Different workplaces 12

Different jobs 14

People who help us 16

Likes and dislikes 18

Places of work 20

Further information for Parents and Teachers 22

Index 24

People who work at our school

There are many people who work at our school. They all do different jobs that make the school run smoothly.

Mr Simmons looks after pupils during break-time.

work school jobs

Our **headteacher** is Mrs Harding.

She is **in charge** of running the school.

She helps **pupils** and teachers if they have problems.

What is the name of your headteacher?

headteacher   in charge   pupils

People who help us learn

There are fourteen classes in our school.

Each class has its own **classteacher**.

Our teacher Miss Taylor takes our lessons and marks our work.

classteacher

Mr Churchill is the librarian at our school.

He works in the library.

He helps us find the books we need.

What other
jobs do librarians do?

librarian library books

Around our school

▶ When **visitors** come to our school, they go to the **front office** first.

◀ The **secretary** in the office helps visitors, sends out letters and collects dinner money.

We eat our dinner in the school dining room.

The dinner staff prepare the meals and serve our food.

They also clean up after dinner.

What other jobs do people do at your school?

dining room   dinner staff   clean up   9

Our local area

There are many other places where people work in our local area.

Suliman's mother is an accountant.

▼ Most of her work is done on a computer.

▲ She works in an office.

accountant computer office

► **Sarah's father is a shopkeeper.**
He owns a toy shop.

▼ **He has a shop assistant who helps him with customers.**

What other sorts of shops do people work in?

Different workplaces

Accountants and shopkeepers work inside.

But some people work outside.

Where do the people in these pictures work?

Can you think of other outside jobs?

inside outside

► **These people drive on the roads.**

What jobs are they doing?

◄ **These people work at the airport.**

What do you think they are doing?

Different jobs

▼ **Some people work during the day ...**

▲ **... and others work at night.**

► **People who work at different times every week are called shift workers.**

Some people work with other people …

… and others work mostly alone.

What jobs can you think of where people work alone?

Here are some buildings
in our local area.

Can you match the people
on the opposite page with
the building they work in?

buildings

It's great working outside but I hate it when it rains!

I enjoy talking to customers, but I don't like working in the evenings.

Most people like some things about their job.

Most people dislike some things about their job.

18 .... like dislike talking evenings

dislikes

I love making people better, but sometimes I can't, and that makes me sad.

I like cooking for children but I don't like cleaning up afterwards!

What sort of job do you think you would like?

sad

Places of work

Here are some people who work in our local area.

Can you describe where each person works?

21

Further information for

Possible Activities

SPREAD ONE

Walk around the school discussing with the children the different jobs that correspond to different areas e.g. a dinner lady works in the canteen preparing meals for the children.

Ask children to list what their headteacher does at the school.

SPREAD TWO

Interview people who work at the school and discuss their different roles, for example a teacher, the caretaker, a dinner lady, the librarian etc.

Interview your own classteacher asking what their favourite lessons are.

Visit the school library and see how the librarian helps to find a book.

SPREAD THREE

Write a letter to the school secretary asking them a question about the school.

List as many different foods as possible that are served in the canteen.

Conduct a survey of the class to find out the favourite and least favourite foods served and plot the results on a graph.

SPREAD FOUR

Invite a local business person to talk about their job and where they work or visit them in their place of work and find out how many people work there and what their different jobs are.

Make a list of children's favourite kinds of shops.

Parents and Teachers

SPREAD FIVE

Make a list of jobs that are based inside and jobs that are based outside. Ask the children to say what their favourite job would be and plot the results on a graph.

SPREAD SIX

Write a list of good and bad points for working during the day and then working at night.

List as many jobs as possible that are done in the day and jobs that are done at night.

Conduct a survey to show the different jobs that children's parents have.

SPREAD SEVEN

Visit a local fire station and talk to the firefighters about the different emergencies they deal with.

Invite a local person in who helps people, for example a doctor, policewoman, or vet and ask them to talk about their job.

SPREAD EIGHT

Ask children to interview their parents/carers asking what they like and dislike about their jobs.

What would the children like and dislike about their favourite/dream job?

SPREAD NINE

Take photographs of buildings where people work and describe who would work there.

Further Information

BOOKS

FOR CHILDREN

Places We Share by Sally Hewitt (Franklin Watts 2000)

Schools by Sally Hewitt (Franklin Watts 2000)

Street by Sally Hewitt (Franklin Watts 2000)

Where We Live by Sally Hewitt (Franklin Watts 2000)

School by Jeff Stanfield (Hodder Wayland 1999)

The Street by Jeff Stanfield (Hodder Wayland 1999)

FOR ADULTS

Handbook of Primary Geography by Roger Carter (Ed) (The Geographical Association 1998)

WEBSITES

http://www.standards.dfee.gov.uk/schemes/geography

http://www.learn.co.uk

http://www.schoolzone.co.uk

Index

a

accountant 10, 12
airport 13

b

books 7
buildings 17

c

class teacher 6
classes 6
cleaning up 9, 19
computer 10
customers 11

d

day workers 14
dining room 9
dinner staff 9

f

food 9
front office 8

h

head teacher 5
helping people 16, 19

l

librarian 7
library 7
likes and dislikes 18-19
local area 10, 17, 20

m

meals 9

n

night workers 14, 18

o

office 10
outside work 12, 13, 18

r

roads 13

s

secretary 8
shift workers 14
shop assistant 11
shopkeeper 11, 12
shops 11

t

teachers 5, 6
toy shop 11

v

visitors 8